THE LITTLE
BLACK BOOK OF
MARTINIS

• The Essential Guide to the King of Cocktails •

NANNETTE STONE

ILLUSTRATED BY KERREN BARBAS

PETER PAUPER PRESS, INC.
WHITE PLAINS, NEW YORK

To Ernest Pacchiana,
for mixing the best martini
and for stirring me

*Peter Pauper Press, Inc. and the author have
used their best efforts to ensure that the ingredients
and directions for each martini are correct.
Nevertheless, we urge readers to use their discretion
and good sense in making these martinis,
and to remember that responsible drinking is
everyone's personal responsibility.*

Designed by Heather Zschock

Illustrations copyright © 2004 Kerren Barbas

Copyright © 2004
Peter Pauper Press, Inc.
202 Mamaroneck Avenue
White Plains, NY 10601
All rights reserved
ISBN 978-0-88088-569-0
Printed in Hong Kong
14 13 12 11

Visit us at www.peterpauper.com

THE LITTLE
BLACK BOOK OF
MARTINIS

CONTENTS

introduction

WARNING!

Martinis don't pull punches.
Pace yourself. Never drink and drive,
never promise anything to anyone
after the second drink, and don't
try to set your martini on fire.

MARTINI MYSTIQUE

The martini (a.k.a. The Silver Bullet, The Cold War, White Lightning, Olive Soup, and See-Through) is not just a drink. It is the soul of cocktail—a liquid icon. It is a transparent razzle-dazzle concoction that implies glamour, style, and edgy wit. Though a martini enjoys a quiet evening at home, it gets invited to all the right parties, sports the most elegant accessories, and is surrounded by devoted movie stars, high rollers, statesmen and literary pundits. From its humble gin and vermouth beginnings, this at first abrasive little drink has been polished, praised, decorated, and lifted to nearly legendary status. Without prejudice it plays muse to heroes, hedonists, rascals, and poets.

*I think I had it in the back of my mind
that I wanted to sound like a dry martini.*

Paul Desmond of the Dave Brubeck Quartet,
when asked about the sound of his sax

When I have one Martini,
I feel bigger, wiser, taller.
When I have the second,
I feel superlative.
When I have more, there's
no holding me.

William Faulkner

*All I ever did was supply a demand
that was pretty popular.*

Al Capone, bootlegger/gangster

WHAT'S IN A MARTINI?

FOR THE PURIST, a martini is always icy cold gin with dry vermouth, served in a long stemmed, cone shaped glass. It may be garnished with a ribbon of fresh lemon peel or an olive skewered on a pick—but it is an otherwise plain, naked, honest drink. One may experiment endlessly with brand names, how to get it cold enough, and the proportion of gin to vermouth. But switch to vodka, add flavor, or even change the garnish—and the reverent traditionalist believes that the martini loses its identity and dissolves into a sea of ordinary cocktails.

VODKATINIS AND FAUX-TINIS. Non-traditional martini lovers, now the majority, often prefer to replace the briskly aromatic gin with strong but invisible vodka. That makes it a vodkatini. Unlike gin with its spicy juniper presence, vodka blends easily with

almost any flavor. Thanks to vodka's accom-
modating nature (much to the chagrin of
those who hold the minimal martini sacred),
the new martini incarnations are often hot,
sweet, fruity, herbal, floral, candied, and
wildly decorated. Modern martinis, faux or
no, often have good taste and very pretty legs
(the filmy rivulets that adhere to the inside
of the glass, as gravity pulls the liquid back
down into the bowl).

"What hit me?" asks Nora Charles
"That last martini," says Nick Charles

From the movie *The Thin Man*

FLUX IT

FLUID IN EVERY SENSE OF THE WORD,
the martini reinvents itself to reflect the fan-
tasies and aspirations of each generation. As
a result, martini lore has become a blurry
mixture of history, mythology, fact, and

intentional embellishment. There is inspired and passionate controversy about martini's every aspect: its beginnings, correct ingredients, proper preparation, merits, and dangers. Even people who don't drink martinis often have strong opinions about them. An oft-told joke is that people who spend time in the wilderness (for example, Canadian Mounties, spelunkers and jungle explorers) should carry martini kits—in case they get lost or in trouble. This is because mixing a martini always ensures that someone will appear out of thin air to tell them they are doing it all wrong.

Martinis . . . have a muting effect on
the constant ringing in my ears, and as
five o'clock approaches, my thoughts
turn toward the elixir of quietude.
Gin stops the bell from tolling.

E. B. White

Gin and vodka, the martini's main ingredients, were born out of medical necessity, but grew popular because of the taste and the buzz. But to make a martini, one of them had to be mixed with…

VERMOUTH

Vermouth is an aid to the digestion; it purifies the blood, induces sound slumber, and rejoices the heart.

Leonardo Fioravanti (16th century)

VERMOUTH WAS BORN MORE THAN 300 YEARS AGO in Italy, but its name is German  and comes from the word for wormwood—"welmut," an ancient remedy for intestinal worms, jaundice, and rheumatism. The earliest versions were sweet red dessert drinks made from blends of wormwood flowers, juniper, bitter orange peel, cloves, cinnamon, nutmeg, coriander, mace, marjoram, brandy, white wine, and tree bark. People believed vermouth had

healing powers, and quenched their thirst with it rather than drink their often polluted water. When French vermouth was first imported to New York in the mid 1800s, it was sold primarily in apothecary shops.

Today, all vermouths—dry, sweet, and half-sweet—are white wines infused with secret blends of herbs and spices, and then fortified with alcohol, sugar, and caramel.

DRY VERMOUTH (also referred to as French vermouth) is pale gold in color and has only a touch of sugar. It is the crucial ingredient that transforms plain gin or vodka (voilà) into a dry martini.

SWEET VERMOUTH (sometimes called Italian) can be white (bianco) or may be colored red (rosso). It is three times as sweet as dry vermouth.

HALF-SWEET (SEMI-SWEET) VERMOUTH is less sugary than sweet vermouth, is the spiciest of the three, and can be red or white.

ORIGINAL GIN

GIN, ONCE CALLED "GENEVER," is a mixture of grain alcohol and juniper berry oil, originally concocted by a 17th-century Dutch medical professor to treat kidney disorders. This walloping strong medicine was cheap, tasty, and easy to produce. It seemed good for stomach aches, gout, and gallstones, and in no time at all it became exceedingly popular. British troops developed a taste for what they called "Dutch Courage" during the Thirty Years' War, and found they could buy it from chemists when they returned to

England. Dutch settlers, on the way to the new colonies, did not leave home without it.

> *Gin and water is the source*
> *of all my inspiration.*
>
> Lord Byron

To boost her economy, England in the late 17th century encouraged the production of distilleries to take advantage of surplus wheat and barley. Gin (called "mother's milk" because it was served warm, sweetened, and in milk) became a sort of currency and was even doled out on payday to compensate workers for their labor. Within 20 years public drunkenness was blatant, and 50 years of government sanctions imposed to correct "mother's ruin" only caused riots, corruption, and foul gin. After the regulations

 were dropped, a more sober society and reputable distilleries prevailed. But it took more than another century for gin to clear its name.

By the 1920s, high quality gin flowed freely, and without stain, on the classy Cunard cruises between London and New York. And, by the '30s (despite Prohibition), martinis and the cocktail hour (something new to do between tea time and dinner) were all the rage on both sides of the Atlantic.

Today you can find two types of gin on the shelf:

The full bodied, malt flavored and highly aromatic HOLLAND GIN is closest to the early Dutch formula and is most often taken alone on ice.

LONDON DRY GIN is the usual choice for mixing dry martinis and other cocktails.

VODKA
(THE INTERLOPER)

> Pulkheria Ivanovna: *Here is vodka*
> *infused with St. John's wort and sage,*
> *for when the small of your back or*
> *shoulder hurts. This one has thistle.*
> *It's just right for the ringing in your ears*
> *and cold sores. This vodka from peach*
> *pits? Swallow some after you've*
> *bumped your head and the lump*
> *disappears right under your hand.*

Nikolai Gogol, *Old World Landowners*

IN THE 12TH CENTURY, "vodka" (a Russian
endearment meaning "little water") was a
crude anesthetic and disinfectant made from
Polish or Russian rye. But by the end of the

14th century people began to appreciate its intoxicating effects. Russians were so convinced that the drink contained a divine spirit that they passed it around in gallon-sized jugs at religious ceremonies. In church, nobody dared turn down a drink—that would be impious.

In time, the professionally manufactured versions, refined from wheat, barley, and mostly corn, became very highly esteemed, and by the early 17th century every imperial banquet started with some bread and vodka. Meanwhile, the peasants figured out how to make a crude home brew with cheap potatoes so that everyone could afford to drink. And everyone did.

Russia indulged her tipsy citizenry until World War I, when she wanted her soldiers sober for battle. Official efforts to suppress vodka consumption during and after the war barely made a dent, and the sobering educational programs of the '20s were abandoned when 10 years later Stalin ordered the re-expansion of vodka production to pump up the revenues needed for defense. Soldiers in the Red Army in World War II were not only allowed to drink, but were actually issued standard government vodka rations.

Vodka wasn't used much in the United States until Smirnoff came on the scene in 1930. Then, in a marketing coup, Smirnoff paid to have James Bond drink only vodka martinis in the 1967 movie version of *Casino Royale*, and the demand for it skyrocketed. Today, vodka has all but surpassed gin at the martini bar in the United States, and it is still the favorite spirit of Russia and Eastern Europe.

"Vot kak!"

That's Russian for "Gadzooks!"

MARRIAGE
AMERICAN STYLE

You can no more keep a
martini in the refrigerator than
you can keep a kiss there.
The proper union of gin and
vermouth is . . . one of the
happiest marriages on earth,
and one of the shortest lived.

Bernard DeVoto

history

If the Lord hadn't intended us to have a three-martini lunch, then why do you suppose He put all those olive trees in the Holy Land?

Former House Speaker Jim Wright

WILL THE REAL FIRST MARTINI MAKER PLEASE STAND UP?

AS SOON AS GIN AND VERMOUTH GOT HITCHED, a martini was born in America, but to tell the truth, nobody can be sure who delivered the first one. Perhaps, like many concepts pushing their way into consciousness, the martini sprang simultaneously from several minds and in different geographic locations.

> *[The martini is] . . . the supreme American gift to world culture.*
>
> Bernard DeVoto

Some say "Professor" Jerry Thomas midwived the first martini—in San Francisco, circa 1850, for a miner on his way to Martinez, California. When his customer slapped a gold nugget onto the bar along with a request for something special, he got a "Martinez," prototype for the "Martini." This recipe was published, along with 23 other recipes, in Professor Thomas's 1887 edition of *The Bartender's Guide*—the first bartender's manual.

. . . the only American invention
as perfect as a sonnet.

H. L. Mencken

PROFESSOR JERRY THOMAS'S MARTINEZ

Use small bar glasses
One dash bitters
Two dashes maraschino
One wine glass vermouth (sweet vermouth)
Two small lumps of ice
One pony (one ounce) Old Tom Gin

Shake up thoroughly and strain into a large "cocktail" glass (then shaped more like a wine glass).

Put a quarter of a slice of lemon in the glass and serve.

If the guest prefers it very sweet, add two dashes of gum syrup.

KINDRED SPIRITS. Today's Martini and Martinez are colder, neater drinks, not nearly as sweet as their father, but the family resemblance is obvious.

THE CLASSIC MARTINI

3 parts gin (or vodka)
1 part dry vermouth

Shake in or stir over a half filled container of cracked ice, and strain into a cocktail glass. Garnish with an olive or a twist of lemon.

A plaque in Martinez, California, credits the bartender Julio Richelieu with making the first martini in 1870. It claims that a miner, who had traded a pouch of gold for whiskey to fill an empty bottle, decided he'd been shortchanged, whereupon Richelieu dumped gin, vermouth, orange, and bitters into a glass to make up the perceived difference. Plop! Was that an olive? The new drink was christened "The Martinez."

MARTINEZ

4 parts gin
2 parts dry vermouth
1 part triple sec
1 dash orange bitters

Stir all ingredients with ice and strain into a cocktail glass. Drop a cherry in it.

The *Oxford English Dictionary* tells us that the word "martini" came from "Martini and Rossi," an early brand of vermouth used in martini recipes. The Italian company, then called Martini e Sola, shipped its first 100 cases of red vermouth to New York in 1871. That's much too late to have been poured into the first Martinez cocktail, but not too late to slur a lot of "nezes" into "nis."

Or should we believe the Brits, some of whom insist that the name came from the Martini & Henry rifles, used by England's army between 1871 and 1891, because they had such an almighty kick?

Others insist that the martini is an East Coast phenomenon, invented in 1911 specially for John D. Rockefeller by a bartender named Martini di Arma di Taggia at New York City's Knickerbocker Hotel. Newcomer or not, it was here that the martini first rubbed shoulders with Wall Street power and began to insinuate itself into big deals made with handshakes over lunch.

THE ROCKEFELLER

One part London dry gin
One part Italian dry vermouth
Splash of orange bitters

Stir with cracked ice and strain into a chilled cocktail glass. Garnish with lemon peel and an olive.

In a drink lineup, the antique Daisy Gin Cocktail (made with gin, Curaçao, simple syrup, soda, and lemon juice) looks a little like a modern martini. "Daisy" meant "fabulous" in the Victorian era. Why not make Daisy a contender? And just when did the cherry garnish turn into an olive? Was it really an olive that Julio Richelieu threw into his California Martinez or should New York City bartender Robert Agneau get credit for first using olives to disguise bad Prohibition gin?

There isn't enough evidence to make us swallow any one of those martini stories whole, but why let facts stand in the way? Do we ask Santa Claus, Paul Bunyan, or the tooth fairy for documentation?

McMurphy: That's right Mr. Martini, there is an Easter Bunny.

From the movie *One Flew Over the Cuckoo's Nest*

THE MARTINI EVOLUTION

FOR DECADES "MARTINEZ," "MARTINE," AND "MARTINI" were interchangeable terms, while the drink remained a sweet and pungent, straw colored liquid with a couple of precious ice cubes floating on top. But as the world turned, martinis kept turning into different drinks. By the turn of the century, a "martini" was always called a "martini," and by that time the name stood for a transparent drink made of half gin and half dry vermouth. Sometime around 1915, refrigerators started to replace ice boxes, drinks started getting colder, and gin dominated the vermouth by a ratio of 2 to 1.

The reign of tears is over. . . .
Men will walk upright now, women
will smile, and the children will laugh.
Hell will be forever for rent.

Preacher Billy Sunday, to a crowd of 10,000
people at midnight, on the eve of Prohibition

[The 1920s came in] with a bang of
bad booze, flappers with bare legs,
jangled morals and wild weekends.

Hoagy Carmichael

The parties were bigger . . . the pace
was faster . . . the morals were looser.

F. Scott Fitzgerald

THE MARTINI GOES INTO HIDING

PROHIBITION (1920-1933) WAS MEANT TO LEGISLATE AMERICA INTO A STATE OF TEETOTALING VIRTUE. It did little to suppress booze, because alcohol just ducked into "speakeasies" and "blind pigs" that by all appearance looked like florists' shops, lobbies, or even funeral parlors. Inside, gin flowed abundantly, because it was the cheapest, easiest, and quickest alcohol to produce. It was badly made, but a little flavoring covered that "bathtub" taste, and the forbidden fruit was forgiven its raw quality. Concealing alcohol became quite a game. People drank their gin out of teacups and kept it hidden in hip flasks, false books, coconut shells and hot water bottles. The now familiar martini glass with its wide rim was especially designed for use in illegal clubs to make for a quick disposal of the evidence. In case of a raid—"three gulps and it's gone." Under Prohibition, alcohol use soared and dancing girls, organized crime, jazz, gamblers, smugglers, illicit sex, cigarettes, and sin thrived. "The noble experiment" had backfired.

I don't make jokes—I just watch the government and report the facts.

Will Rogers

During Prohibition, American tourists were especially happy to get good gin for a decent martini abroad, and they introduced Europeans to their special flavored cocktail. In Paris a martini was called a "Gin and It," and in London clubs, it became popular to add a dash of licorice absinthe (now an illegal substance) to the mix. This made both the martini and the minds of the patrons extraordinarily cloudy.

After the first glass you see things as you wish they were. After the second, you see things as they are not. Finally you see things as they really are, and that is the most horrible thing in the world.

Oscar Wilde, on absinthe

Ernest Hemingway drank absinthe long after it was made illegal in most parts of the world. Many suspect that he was on absinthe when he went running with the bulls.

WHEN IT WAS OVER, OVER HERE. Immediately after FDR signed the act repealing Prohibition on December 6, 1933, he put down his pen and said, "What the nation needs now is a drink." He then personally mixed America's first post-Prohibition legal martini in the White House.

FDR'S MARTINI

1 part gin
1/2 part vermouth
1 teaspoon olive brine

Roosevelt shook his martinis with cracked ice, added one olive, rubbed the glass rim with a lemon peel and imbibed to "relieve his back pain." His staff said he was a sloppy mixer because he was apt to dump orange juice, grapefruit juice, or anisette into his drinks too. He liked to do his international negotiating over shared martinis.

It is cold on the stomach.

Stalin, on FDR's martini, at the 1943 Teheran Conference

. . . America's lethal weapon.

Nikita Khrushchev, on the even stronger
martini Eisenhower gave him

BIG SCREEN MARTINIS

The camera loves a martini.
Even when it is only an extra or
a prop, it can steal the show.

1934: In **The Thin Man**, William
Powell (Nick) and Myrna Loy (Nora)
played the parts of sexy, sassy sleuths.
Nick did naughty things like shoot
ornaments off the Christmas tree when
he was tanked. Nora, rather than
becoming annoyed, just tried to catch
up with Nick when she discovered him
drunk on six martinis. (To the waiter)
"Six martinis." (To Nick) "You're not
going to have anything on me."

1936: In **My Man Godfrey**, David Niven played the part of a butler who sneaked sips of martini from his employer's serving tray.

1942: In **The Major and the Minor**, Robert Benchley (as Mr. Osbourne) gets to deliver the best line in the show: "Why don't you get out of that wet coat and into a dry martini," he says to Ginger Rogers (as Susan Applegate), in a manner halfway between wry and lecherous.

1945: "Most men lead lives of quiet desperation. I can't take quiet desperation. What better reason for that

second martini?" explained Ray Milland, playing an alcoholic having trouble staying sober in **The Lost Weekend**.

1945: In Noel Coward's **Blithe Spirit**, people dress for dinner, dangle cigarettes from holders and balance their martinis between quips. "Anyone can write books, but it takes an artist to make a dry martini."

1950: That was a dry martini Bette Davis knocked back before she delivered her famous line: "Fasten your seatbelts. It's going to be a bumpy night," in **All About Eve**.

1954: In **Sabrina**, Larrabee tries to fish out the last olive in the jar for his martini, but gives up and dumps the martini fixings into the jar.

1959: In Alfred Hitchcock's **North by Northwest**, Cary Grant wheels and deals over a few martinis.

HOW DRY I AM

(After Prohibition)

PARTYERS DIDN'T GIVE UP THEIR TASTE for gin when it became legal. Throughout the 1930s, '40s, and '50s, the gin just got better and the martinis just got stronger.

The earliest martinis were made with equal portions of gin and sweet vermouth, and a request for a dry martini meant: "use the drier (white) vermouth." But gradually white vermouth became the standard unspoken order and "dry" came to mean "use less vermouth." A four to one ratio became a medium dry martini; a six to one ratio, a dry martini; an eight to one ratio, a very dry martini; and an arid martini called for a ratio of twelve to one.

At some point, a taste for very little vermouth became associated with being in the know,

 tough, and attractively seasoned. Robert Benchley insisted that the recipe for an ideal martini was "three parts gin and enough vermouth to take away that ghastly watery look." Hemingway's martini had a ratio of 15 to 1, and was named The Montgomery after the British field marshal who liked those odds on the battlefield. Then came the Bone Dry Martini (16 to 1), followed by the practice of simply sloshing a little vermouth around in the glass and tossing it out before adding the gin.

Still dissatisfied with the "dry" in their drinks, people used droppers made by Hammacher Schlemmer and silver syringes made by Gorham to titrate tiny drops of vermouth into their gin. And some just misted a bit of vermouth over the tops of their glasses with an atomizer.

THE NO VERMOUTH MARTINI

Churchill was said to have just looked at the bottle of vermouth across the room and nodded toward France while pouring out his gin. This pure gin beverage did not (according to his own report) adversely affect him.

I have taken more out of alcohol than alcohol has taken out of me.

Winston Churchill

THE WINSTON CHURCHILL

2 parts London dry gin
Garnish with a lemon peel

Stir gin in ice to the chorus of *Rule Britannia*, and whisper "France" before straining the mixture into a shallow glass.

Rule Britannia! Britannia rules the waves.
Britons never, never, never shall be slaves.

IMAGINARY VERMOUTH

BARTENDERS WHO ADMIT to serving pure gin when asked for a dry martini still get drinks returned to the bar with the complaint that they contain too much vermouth. A few claim that adding just a drop of vodka to an otherwise all gin martini makes it seem still drier.

I'd like a dry martini, Mr. Quoc, a very dry
martini. A very dry, arid, barren, desiccated,
veritable dustbowl of a martini. I want a
martini that could be declared a disaster area.
Mix me just such a martini.

Hawkeye, in a TV episode of *M.A.S.H.*

Did the Gibson start out wet? The Gibson (a martini sporting one or two pearl onions instead of an olive) may have been created to flatter Charles Dana Gibson, magazine illustrator and creator of the "Gibson Girl." Or maybe the onion was used, as is commonly rumored, to mark the martini impostor (water only) made on the sly for some other Mr. Gibson. This trick made it possible for a teetotaler to put drinking guests at ease, or for a betting man to cheat in drinking contests.

This is an excellent martini—
sort of tastes like it isn't there at all,
just a cold cloud.

Herman Wouk

GIBSON RECIPE

2 parts gin (or vodka)
0 to 1 part dry vermouth (according to taste)
Two pearl onions speared with any sort of pick

Shake in or stir over half filled container of cracked ice, and strain into glass. Garnish with onions.

THE MARTINI DROP-OUT

THE MARTINI WAS THE UNCONTESTED AMERICAN CHAMPION OF DRINKS UNTIL THE LATE '60S, AND '70S, when young people "tuned in" to pot and wine. Tie-dye, long hair, denim, and anti-establishment attitudes were in. Thin ties, red meat, girdles—and martinis—were turn-offs.

Martinis were country club drinks, uptight and strait-laced. Nixon drank them. Parents drank them. They were for boardrooms and men in suits. "Fern bar" drinks (beverages for washing down drugs) and "girl drinks" (a term applied to drinks made for those who do not like the taste of alcohol) were preferred. Martinis were civilized and citified—all wrong for campouts and rock concerts. You'd have to wear a cocktail dress or a tie to drink one.

Nixon drank his "In and Out Martinis" as the Watergate investigation drove him out of the presidency. His billionaire buddy Bebe Rebozo prepared them for him with perfection.

THE IN AND OUT

Slosh a little vermouth around in a cocktail shaker full of ice and spill it out right away. Then pour in the gin, stir, and strain.

Frank Sinatra became friends with the "gorgeously indifferent" Dean Martin (a.k.a. Dino and Dag) during the filming of Some Came Running. *Together with Sammy Davis Jr., they were the core of the Las Vegas Rat Pack, a hard partying bunch of performers who, martinis prominently in hand, cornered the market in irreverence, swagger and raffishly cool talent. Peter Lawford, Joey Bishop, Shirley MacLaine, Juliet Prowse, Angie Dickinson, Tony Curtis and Janet Leigh, and even Jack Kennedy, sometimes hung out with this crowd.*

THE MARTINI WAR

JACK KENNEDY first pointed an accusatory finger at the martini lunch because he hated long business meetings over meals. George McGovern decided to take up the cause and railed against the evil two-martini lunch, and in the '70s abstemious President Jimmy Carter waged war on fat cats who took big tax deductions for three-martini lunches. "Three-martini lunches!" became a battle cry, and the martini, once a lubricant for political as well as business negotiations, was now judged greedy, immoral, and unfit for public service.

The three-martini lunch is the epitome of American efficiency. Where else can you get an earful, a bellyful, and a snootful at the same time?

Gerald Ford

THE RETURN OF THE MARTINI

THE MARTINI BARELY SURVIVED INTO THE '80S. A few old timers still ordered plain vodka or gin, with the standard little green olive or chunk of lemon in it, but the pizzazz had fizzled out—and it just wasn't a young people's drink.

Then, out of the blue, a martini stampede thundered in! Hundreds of designer martinis hit the bars all at once, wearing shiny trinkets on their swizzle sticks—poised to seduce the first timers. Come-hither lips looked great sipping from those elegant glass-

es and everyone yearned for a martini experience. Martini was no longer a one-size-fits-all kind of drink; there were flavors to suit every taste. But more than that, it was chic, smart, and sexy to hold one of those sophisticated glasses.

Was this a form of nostalgia? A rebellion against hippie parents? A new wave of self-indulgence? Or, was it just a good excuse to finally get dressed up? The martini initiates, at first lured in by the sweet drinks made out of vodka and juice, learned with practice to appreciate straight vodka and gin martinis. At home and out on the town, the martini was back on top and here to stay.

And everything old is new again.

So, when he looked down into his martini, he was put into a trance by dancing myriads of winking eyes on the surface of his drink. The eyes were beads of lemon oil.

Kurt Vonnegut, Jr., *Breakfast of Champions*

THE HOW-TO'S

TO SHAKE OR TO STIR—THAT IS THE QUESTION. . . . Mixing a martini is some-thing akin to medieval alchemy. The results  are magical and transitory. The same ingredients may yield differ-ent results depending upon such ephemeral variables as the weath-er, the spring in your wrist, the alignment of Jupiter with Venus, or the twinkle in your eye when the gin and vermouth fall giddily into your glass.

A martini should always be stirred, not shaken, so that the molecules lie sensuously on top of one another.

W. Somerset Maugham

Stirrers wouldn't dream of "bruising" their gin by banging it around. They may swirl around a glass stirring rod three or four times to the rhythm of a waltz or some California jazz, and they like to use tall pitchers with pointy lips to hold back the ice. They thrill to the sight of a crystal-clear liquid seen through the prism of white diamond glass. A few sprinkle some drops of club soda onto the ice before adding the other ingredients. It is supposed to encourage the vermouth to cling evenly to the periphery of the glass.

Shakers go for stainless steel instruments with ice strainers in the interest of making the most frigid drink possible. After shaking vigorously for up to 30 times, they shake some more—until their hands hurt from the cold. Only such dynamic motion can properly alter the molecular structure and eliminate what they perceive as an oily mouth feel. They do not find

the tiny bubbles that temporarily make the drink cloudy at all objectionable. To them, the little wisps are like cirrus clouds evaporating in a fair weather sky. The oxygen added from this vigorous agitation sharpens the taste of the aromatics in the gin but has no effect on the taste of vodka.

WHEN JAMES BOND SHOOK

"I never have more than one drink before dinner, but I do like that one to be large and very strong and very cold and very well-made. . . .
This drink is my own invention. I'm going to patent it when I can think of a good name," said James Bond.

From Ian Fleming's novel Casino Royale *(1953)*

Bond decided to name his drink "The Vesper" after a beautiful Russian double agent. Here he gives the recipe:

"A dry martini," he said.
"One. In a deep champagne goblet."
"Oui, monsieur."
"Just a moment. Three measures of Gordon's,
one of vodka, half a measure of Kina Lillet
(a brand of French aperitif).
Shake it very well until it's ice-cold, then add
a large thin slice of lemon-peel. Got it?"

James Bond, in Ian Fleming's novel *Casino Royale*

SCIENCE: THE 007 STUDY. James Bond, a very healthy male specimen with no evidence of heart disease, high blood pressure, or cataracts, shook his martinis. What is the scientific significance, pondered doctors in the Biochemistry Laboratories at The University of Western Ontario, Canada? Whipping out their glass beakers, they stirred and shook identical portions of gin and vermouth and then measured the resultant antioxidant activity in both drinks.

CONCLUSION: Indeed, shaking produced the drink with the most antioxidants, and thus the healthier drink. Since this study took no account of the fact that Mr. Bond used vodka and Kina Lillet (which contains quinine and its own special herbal ingredients), more research is obviously needed.

Yes, but my martini is still dry.
My name is James.

James Bond, in the movie *Never Say Never Again*

GET READY, GET SET— GO COLD

A MARTINI MUST BE COLD—GLACIAL, FRIGID, BONE-CHILLING, ARCTIC COLD. Here's a tip. Think iceberg. Have on hand ten times more ice than you'd expect to need for each martini. Ice is never used twice. Every time you chill a glass, or pour your liquid ingredients over ice, dump the used cubes immediately. Anything that looks wet isn't cold enough.

We have found a way of making ice in the deep freeze in tennis ball tubes that comes out 15 degrees below zero and with glasses frozen too makes the coldest martini in the world . . . [Add] Spanish cocktail onions very crisp and also 14 degrees below zero when they go into the glass.

Ernest Hemingway

Be sure your freezer is pristine. If your water isn't 100% scent-free, either use distilled water in the trays or buy bags of ice from the gro-

cer. No steel balls or funny looking little plastic cubes please.

Chill your glasses in the freezer if possible, or else put them in the sink filled with ice ready to be dumped out and shaken dry at the last minute.

Gin or vodka from the freezer produces a frigid drink with just a drop of melted ice. Room temperature spirits yield a kinder, gentler drink made with up to one-fourth water. Experiment. Vermouth will freeze in the freezer and will lose flavor in the refrigerator. Keep it on the bar shelf—but not for more than three months once opened.

Cocktail shakers from the '30s, shaped like penguins, are considered good luck. Born in tuxedos, these are symbols of success and affluence that never fly away.

Imagine a Great Gatsby party. Pastel lace and pearls . . . beads swinging over the knees of skinny flappers . . . haunting jazz . . . and some martinis mixed in one of those gorgeous silver shakers and served on a silver platter. Guess what they used to cost? In 1930, sterling silver cocktail shakers, bearing the Charter Company leaf mark, sold for $200.00 alone or $725.00 with 12 matching "cocktail cups" and a tray. That shaker set would set you back over $7,000.00 today!

A stainless steel art deco shaker, shaped like a sleek bullet, represented power, speed, and modernization in the '30s. The design remained popular until World War II, when all available metal was channeled into the production of real artillery shells and other armaments for the military.

Norman Bel Geddes, famous artist, stage designer, and industrial inventor, created the streamlined chrome "Manhattan Cocktail Set" in 1937. Worthy of its exhibit in the Metropolitan Museum of Art, this set shows off Bel Geddes's ability to use reflected light to express a mood or an idea. The silvery shaker, tray, and stemware looked as much like icy cold liquid as the martinis that filled them.

the martini bar

I've been terrible at remembering people's names. I once introduced a friend of mine as Martini. Her name was actually Olive.

Tallulah Bankhead

APPARATUS

USE ONLY SPOTLESSLY CLEAN GLASS OR STAINLESS STEEL COCKTAIL SHAKERS, mixing pitchers and utensils. Aluminum and copper can react to some ingredients, particularly those that are citric. Nickel and that Gatsby silver are gorgeous, but be careful—even one smidgen of tarnish remover will completely taint the drink.

The same goes for your measuring spoons, bar strainer, stirring rod, and your 1-1/2 ounce jigger measure.

Don't forget to lay out a can opener, bottle opener, corkscrew, zester, hammer, and a couple of very sharp paring knives on that sterile slicing board. Complete the ensemble with abundant coasters, napkins, and crisp white towels.

GLASSES

USE ONLY THE CLASSIC CONE SHAPED COCKTAIL GLASSES with long stems that keep your fingers from warming the liquid. Stick to the smaller size glasses so drinks won't have time to warm up between sips. If you just love your new oversized martini glasses, then use them first thing in the evening and switch immediately to smaller-sized glasses when the rate of consumption slows down.

Our eyes have become accustomed to restaurant martinis, most often served in 7-ounce glasses rather than the 3-ounce ones of yesteryear. Not only does that make the calorie count zoom from 206 calories to 480

 (even without the olive), it means that your meal can turn into one of those notorious three-martini lunches even before the soup comes.

Martini presentation is a great opportunity for self-expression, so suit yourself. There are thousands of martini glasses to choose from.  Personal style may dictate: expensive Waterford, flea market oddities, or vessels with slouching stems that make you feel inebriated even before you start. Do you like the look of olives but not the taste? How about some hand-painted ones, forever brineless, and permanently fixed to the side of your glass? Have literary aspirations? Get blue ones, like those used in the Algonquin Blue Bar, and think up witty things to say at the next party. Take a risk—it's only money and cupboard space. Just don't insult your martinis by pouring them into plain drinking glasses or that disposable plastic stuff that never feels cold enough.

In the 1920s, a group of New York writers who called themselves the "Vicious Circle" met daily for lunch and drinks at the Algonquin Hotel Round Table. Dorothy Parker, Robert Benchley, George S. Kaufman, Ring Lardner, Alexander Woollcott, and Heywood Broun were among those who exchanged gossip and barbs in the elegant hotel they called "The Gonk." During Prohibition, a friend who kept a still in her room upstairs slipped them gin for martinis.

If I displayed this cup, I might look at it once or twice a week. By using it, I get pleasure from it continually.

Lila Acheson Wallace, on the 4,000-year-old Egyptian cup she used to sip martinis

MEASUREMENTS

Dashes, splashes, shots, pinches, and squeezes are loosely approximated, as follows:

DASH = 1/3 teaspoon or about 10 drops

SPLASH = 1-1/2 teaspoons or about 1/4 ounce

SHOT = about 1-1/2 ounces

PINCH = 1/8 teaspoon or less

SQUEEZE = the juice from 1/6 of a lemon or lime

Jiggers and ponies call for more precise measures:

A JIGGER = 1-1/2 fluid ounces

A PONY = 1 ounce (A double-sided jigger has a 1-ounce cup on the opposite end.)

Other useful equivalents:

3 teaspoons = 1 tablespoon = 1/2 fluid ounce = 15 milliliters

6 teaspoons = 1 ounce = one pony = 2 tablespoons = 30 milliliters

1-1/2 ounces = one jigger = 45 milliliters

16 tablespoons = 1 cup = 8 ounces

GARNISHES—PRETTY PLEASE!

MARTINIS ARE EYE CANDY AS MUCH AS THEY ARE PALATE PLEASERS. Bartenders have built careers on clever and attractive garnishes. All the trimmings, except for pickled ingredients like olives and onions, must be just-picked fresh, vividly colorful, and free of blemishes. If you stick with plain olives, make sure they are plump and beautiful. Remember, there are more than 40 kinds, and you can stuff them with more than pimiento. Poke some anchovy, blue cheese, smoked salmon, shrimp, pistachio nut, caviar, jalapeño, almond, caper, wasabi, or roasted garlic in that hole.

Just lemon? Then why use a stubby little piece of rind if you can carve out a long curly yellow coil? Be creative. Use a cookie cutter to make little citrus rind stars, or carve those peels into the initials of your guests.

> *Happiness is finding two olives in your martini when you're hungry.*
>
> Johnny Carson

Garnishes can be amusing, artistic, collectible, tipsy (marinated in liqueur), creative, tasty, sexy, or silly. Here are a few seen floating through the chic atmosphere of glossy martini bars:

- Grape tomatoes, carved out and stuffed with all the things you might put in olives
- Crystallized violets
- Fresh sprigs of thyme
- Pineapple wedges
- Rosemary twigs

- Chocolate kisses and curls
- Melon balls
- Miniature cobs of corn
- Artichoke hearts
- Green beans
- Watercress
- Tiny eggplants
- Tomato wedges
- Capers on stems
- Fresh nutmeg
- Fruit or rinds cut into the shape of birds
- Walnuts
- Hunks of crystallized ginger
- Onions (pearls), threaded like a tiny string of beads
- Green onions
- Cherries marinated in vermouth
- Fresh strawberries

- Horseradish
- Kumquats
- Chocolate-covered strawberries
- Fresh cherries dangled by the stems over a sip straw
- Pinches of gold dust

- Espresso beans
- Whole mint leaves
- Litchi nuts
- Gum drops
- Gummy worms
- Sugarcoated grapefruit wedges
- Radishes stuffed with olives in order to look like Halloween eyeballs
- Very young dandelion leaves (old ones will be bitter)

If you want to use edible flower petals as a garnish, don't use them straight from garden stores or you may get a dash of pesticide in your mix. Blossoms gathered from the roadside may contain a sprinkle of pollutants.

Picks and swizzles can be plain, humorous, expensive (you can spend up to $90.00 for a pair of silver ones), or edible. Try sugar cane twigs, chocolate straws and cinnamon sticks.

When you want to decorate your glass (with salt, cocoa, coconut, or sprinkles for instance), coat only the outside of the glass so that none falls into the drink. Never wet the rim and just plunk the glass face down.

ONLY THE BEST

Cheat with vodka but not with gin or vermouth.

Always choose the best ingredients you can afford, but keep in mind that the difference between expensive and cheap vodka, unless it is flavored, is mostly a matter of viscosity. Does it slide slowly over the tongue, move right through, or linger on the palate? Once you add anything with a taste to your mixed drink, the kind of vodka you use won't be very important.

Quality gin, on the other hand, is essential. Because it is easy to make gin badly, cheap gin is often bad. Since, unlike the best

 bottle of a first growth wine, the best bottle of gin is probably within your budget, why not choose the best? Gin is highly aromatic; the strong, distinctive

flavor differs quite a bit between brands. Beefeater, Bombay Sapphire, Gordon's, and Tanqueray, for instance, vary greatly in taste.

BOMBAY SAPPHIRE is light and crisp. It is slightly lemony, but on the whole it has a very balanced blend of spices.

TANQUERAY is on the spicy side: fresh, herbal, very complex, and very lingering.

GORDON'S has a hint of juniper up front, followed by coriander. It has a citrus backdrop, and is inexpensive.

BEEFEATER can be described as a juniper up front, spicy, fruity gin. It has a lavender backdrop, is not very complex, and is not very expensive.

The only way to know what appeals to you is to experiment. It is best to compare several gins at one sitting. Order martinis made from several brands of gin and get a little help (drinking them, that is) from your friends. Or talk your local bartender into pouring out mini samples.

Brand name vermouth is not all the same either. Some connoisseurs swear by Martini & Rossi Dry, while others wouldn't dream of using anything but Noilly Pratt Dry. What's your pleasure?

But that's enough of history, lore, pithy quotations, and how-to's. It's time to fix us up that perfect martini—but which one to choose? Here are some satisfying answers to that very question.

recipes

A well-made dry Martini or Gibson,
correctly chilled and nicely served,
has been more often my true friend
than any two-legged creature.

M. F. K. Fisher, food writer

● THE BASIC MARTINIS ●

THE GIN MARTINI

Gin
Dry vermouth to taste:
   4 parts gin to 1 part vermouth is a medium
      dry martini
   6 to 1 is dry
   8 to 1 is very dry
   12 to 1 is an arid martini

Shake or stir, with cracked ice. Strain this blueblood liquid into a cold martini glass. Garnish with a green olive or a lemon twist. Hold the glass by the slender stem with one hand and cup your other hand under the base. Now you've got sophistication in the palm of your hand.

THE VODKATINI

Vodka
Dry vermouth to taste:
  4 parts vodka to 1 part vermouth is a
    medium dry vodkatini
  6 to 1 is dry
  8 to 1 is very dry
  12 to 1 is an arid vodkatini

Without aromatics (which get sharp when shaken), vodka stays relaxed no matter how hard you slam it around. If this is what you want, be sure to say "vodkatini" when you order out, or the bar may send you a juniper surprise.

THE SWEET MARTINI

Gin or vodka
Sweet vermouth to taste (commonly 1 part vermouth to 3 parts gin)
Lemon slice

After you strain the liquid into a chilled glass, rub the rim with a big slice of lemon and then hook the lemon over the edge. The squeeze is a last minute act. Balance the taste by adding a few drops of fresh juice just before you lift your glass.

● MARTINIS A TO Z ●

THE ABSOLUTE MARTINI

5 parts vodka
1 part triple sec
Splash of fresh lemon juice
Dash of orange bitters

Shake or stir the ingredients—with plenty of conviction and cracked ice. Strain into a chilled cocktail glass. A martini exudes an air of confidence—absolutely!

ALLEN COCKTAIL

4 parts gin
1 part maraschino liqueur
1/2 teaspoon fresh lemon juice

Feeling tense? Agitate those spirits over ice and wrench them through the strainer into your glass. Squeeze lemon juice over the top. Loosen up.

ALLIES COCKTAIL

4 parts gin
1 part dry vermouth
1/2 teaspoon Jägermeister

Stir the ingredients over cracked ice and strain into your cocktail glass. Multiply that formula and make a pitcherful. Now invite some friends over. Or don't.

APPLE PIE MARTINI

6 parts vanilla vodka
1 part Calvados
1 part dry vermouth

Shake ingredients with ice and strain. Stick tiny chunks of apple, blueberries, and bits of vanilla wafer on top of a long wooden pick. Make sure it is long enough to keep that red, white, and blue decoration high and dry. Mom never made pie like this—or did she?

APPLETINI

1 part vodka
1 part apple liqueur

Use sea salt crystals to coat the rim of a chilled glass. Shake and strain the liquid ingredients through ice, and garnish with a pretty, tempting slice of apple. Put it on a tray next to some cheddar cheese or warm baked Brie and carry it out into the garden. That's paradise!

ARTILLERY

3 parts gin
1 part red vermouth
Dash of bitters

Shake or stir the ingredients with cracked ice and strain into cocktail glass. Sip slowly. It has a real kick, but it is not a shot.

BARNUM

1 part apricot brandy
2 or 3 dashes bitters
2 parts gin
1 dash lemon juice

Now for the drum roll: Swing the combined ingredients in the shaker high over your shoulder and then strain into glass. Daringly garnish with a slice of apricot, and fly high.

BEADLESTONE

1 part white vermouth
1 part excellent scotch

Shake or stir the ingredients with cracked ice and strain into cocktail glass. What's a nice scotch like you doing in a place like this?

BERRY MARTINI

4 parts vodka
1 part cranberry juice
1 part Chambord liqueur

Shake with cracked ice and strain into a chilled martini glass. Garnish with a lemon twist.

It's sweet and berry delicious!

BLACK-OUT MARTINI

4 parts vodka
2 parts black raspberry liqueur
1 part blue Curaçao

Shake or stir over ice and strain into a cocktail glass. Stick two huge black raspberries on a pick and sink them into your drink. If you lose electricity and can't watch TV, light a candle and take one of these martinis to bed with you along with your significant other and watch the sparks fly!

BLENTON

2 parts gin
1 part dry vermouth
Dash Angostura Bitters

Shake or stir over ice and strain into a cocktail glass. Make this drink so cold it causes frostbite. Don't dress it up with anything. Stunning!

BLONDIE

3 parts strawberry vodka
Splash of Grand Marnier
Orange garnish

Shake or stir over ice and strain into a cocktail glass. Place a wheel of sliced orange on the edge.

BLOODHOUND

2 or more ounces gin or vodka
Splash dry vermouth
Splash sweet vermouth
Splash strawberry liqueur
1 large strawberry

This old timer has been around since the 1930s. Serve it with a plate of strawberries that have been marinated for about an hour in strawberry liqueur.

BLUE VELVET MARTINI

6 parts vodka
1 part blue Curaçao
Dash of Rose's lime juice

Stir with cracked ice and strain into a chilled cocktail glass. Garnish with a slice of lemon.

BOOMERANG

2 ounces gin
1 ounce white vermouth
Splash of maraschino liqueur
Dash of bitters
Kiwi wheel for garnish

Shake or stir the gin and other ingredients with cracked ice, and strain into cocktail glass. Garnish with kiwi wheel. See if you find yourself coming back for more.

BRONX TALE-TINI

3 parts gin
1 part dry vermouth
1 part sweet vermouth

After mixing with ice and straining into a glass, top with a thin layer of orange juice. Now tell me a story.

BUCKEYE

Gin
Vermouth to taste
A black olive replaces the green one.

Shake or stir the gin and vermouth with cracked ice and strain into a cocktail glass. Sink the olive. Some people, especially in Ohio, keep real buckeye nuts in their pockets to bring good luck in money, love, and football.

CAJUN MARTINI

2 parts pepper vodka
Dry vermouth to taste

Shake or stir. Garnish with a jalapeño pepper or olive stuffed with jalapeño.

Want even more fire in your ice? Pull the pimiento out of the olive and replace it with a dab of horseradish, wasabi, or habanero pepper.

William Holden used to say "Warm up the ice cubes," when he wanted a drink. Once, as a practical joke, he set fire to a martini and called it the Hot Martini. Don't try this at home.

CARIBBEAN

2 parts white rum
1 part dry vermouth
Juice of half an orange

Stir with cracked ice and strain into a cocktail glass.

CHOCOLATINI

5 parts vodka (regular or vanilla)
1 part dark chocolate liqueur
1 part white chocolate liqueur

Shake or stir over cracked ice and strain into your icy martini glass. Garnish with a chocolate kiss.

LOGIC: Martinis make you feel good. Chocolate makes you feel good. Chocolate has potassium. Potassium is good for you. Have another one.

COSMOPOLITAN

2 parts vodka
1 part triple sec
Juice of half a lime
Cranberry juice

Pull bottle of vodka out of the freezer, pour all ingredients except cranberry juice over cracked ice, and shake it, shake it, shake it! Then strain into a sexy, thin-rimmed glass. Splash in enough cranberry juice to match the blush on your cheek. Drape it with a thin sliver of lime. After the first sip, slide your tongue seductively between your lips while gazing into your partner's eyes. This is what is called a conjugal martini.

DAISY GIN MARTINI

2 parts gin
Splash of Curaçao
1 tablespoon simple syrup
2 parts club soda
Squeeze of fresh lemon juice

It's best to stir this one. It is a sort of gin spritzer, and it's very refreshing.

Dirty Martinis. A Dirty Martini is a gin or vodka martini with any amount of vermouth and a little olive brine. A Filthy Martini is one with extra olive brine. A Filthy Wet Martini has extra brine and extra vermouth. There is also a Moldy Martini in which the pimiento is removed and replaced with hand-packed blue cheese. Not moved? Then how about a Martini Poo?

DIRTY POO MARTINI

2 parts vodka
2 parts coconut rum
Splash of cranberry juice
Splash of mango juice
Dash of Cointreau

Shake ingredients over ice and strain into a cocktail glass.

EL PRESIDENTE

3 parts Gold Label rum
1 part dry vermouth
1 dash grenadine

Stir with cracked ice and strain into cocktail glass. Garnish with cherry or orange peel.

EMERALD FOREST

1 part gin
Dash of white crème de menthe
Dash of green crème de menthe

Stir ingredients with cracked ice and strain into a cocktail glass. Garnish with a sprig of mint.

Admire the enchanting color—greener than sea waves, shinier than wet emeralds sparkling in the sand.

EMERALD MARTINI

12 parts gin
4 parts dry vermouth
1 part Chartreuse liqueur

Stir with cracked ice and strain into a chilled cocktail glass.

Garnish with a twist of lemon or lime peel.

It's a gem!

ESPRESSO MARTINI

3 parts vodka (regular or vanilla flavored)
1 part crème de cacao

Stir with cracked ice and strain into a chilled cocktail glass.

Garnish with 2 or 3 espresso beans.

FARMER'S COCKTAIL

4 parts gin
1 part red vermouth
1 part white vermouth
Quite a few dashes of Angostura Bitters

Stir with cracked ice and strain into a cocktail glass. Garnish with a slender slice of rhubarb and a strawberry.

It was a long way from the farm to the speakeasy, so country folks had to make their own booze and merriment during Prohibition. Stills rigged up behind the barn made gin that needed fixin'. Pour some more bitters. And now for the entertainment . . .

FIFTY/FIFTY

1 part gin
1 part dry vermouth
Olive garnish

Stir over cracked ice and strain into your glass. This is what people drank in the early 1900s. The odds are better than even that you'll like it!

FINO

3 parts gin
1 part dry sherry
Lemon twist garnish

Stir your best ingredients over ice and strain into a cocktail glass. Fine!

"Fino" means fine.

FLIRTINI

During a party at Guastavino's, Sarah Jessica Parker took one sip of this colorful, easy to swallow drink, and promptly dubbed it the "Flirtini."

1 ounce raspberry vodka
Lime, pineapple, and cranberry juices to taste
Raspberries
Champagne

Splash some fresh lime, pineapple and cranberry juices over vodka. Muddle some raspberries in the bottom of the glass. (Raspberry syrup can be substituted.)

Pour your best champagne on top. Garnish with a mint sprig and wink at that attractive stranger.

GIN AND IT

2 ounces gin
Italian sweet vermouth
Lemon zest

Pour enough vermouth into a pre-chilled glass to coat the sides when the glass is twirled. Add the cold gin and a small sliver of lemon zest. (That's the oily outer layer of peel. Remove every bit of white pulp.)

Happiness is a good martini,
a good meal, a good cigar and a
good woman . . . or a bad woman,
depending on how much
happiness you can stand.

George Burns

GLASNOST

3 parts vodka
1 part peppermint schnapps

Shake or stir with cracked ice and strain into a chilled cocktail glass. Glasnost is Russian for "open." Feel like talking?

GOLDEN MARTINI

5 parts yellow gin
1 part dry vermouth

Stir with cracked ice and strain into a chilled cocktail glass.

Made with yellow, aged gin—this is a superior drink.

GOLF MARTINI

4 parts gin
1 part vodka
4 dashes Angostura Bitters

Shake or stir with cracked ice and strain into
a chilled cocktail glass. Drop in a little white
cocktail onion. That's a hole in one!

GORDON

5 parts Gordon Gin
1 part dry Duff Gordon sherry

Stir with ice and strain into a chilled cocktail glass.

GRAND DUCHESS

3 parts vodka
1 part Gold Label rum
2 parts lime juice
1 part grenadine

Shake with ice and strain into a chilled cocktail glass.

GREEN TEA MARTINI

1 part green tea, chilled (or a pinch of the powdered version)
2 parts lemon vodka
1 teaspoon Cointreau
1 teaspoon simple syrup
Orange twist

Pour green tea, vodka, Cointreau, and simple syrup into a shaker with ice. Shake and strain into your glass. Add orange twist.

GYPSY QUEEN

4 parts vodka
1 part Benedictine
1 dash orange bitters

Shake with ice and strain into a chilled cocktail glass.

It's useless to hold a person to anything he says while he's in love, drunk, or running for office.

Shirley MacLaine

THE HARD BODY MARTINI

(Okay, so it's a Jell-O shot in a cock-tail glass)

1 package lemon Jell-O
1/2 cup boiling water
1/8 cup vodka
1/8 cup peach liqueur
Maraschino cherries

Pour Jell-O mix into boiling water; stir until dissolved. Add vodka and peach liqueur. Stir, and pour into martini glasses. Place a cherry in each drink. Refrigerate, or chill drinks in the freezer for even less jiggle.

Let's all drink gin and make wry faces.

Spoken by Bob Hope, in the movie
The Cat and the Canary

HAVANA CLUB

3 parts Gold Label rum
1 part sweet vermouth
1 dash bitters

Stir with ice and strain into cocktail glass.

Garnish with cherry.

HAWAIIAN MARTINI

4 parts vodka
2 parts Midori
1 part pineapple juice

Shake with ice and strain into a
chilled cocktail glass.

Garnish with pineapple wedge.

HOLLYWOOD MARTINI

1 ounce gin
Splash of dry vermouth
Splash of Goldwasser liqueur

Stir the gin and dry vermouth with cracked ice, strain into cocktail glass, and then pour the Goldwasser gently on top. That shine on top is real gold leaf. Smile—it won't stick to your teeth.

HONG KONG

5 parts gin
1 part dry vermouth
1 teaspoon sugar syrup
1 teaspoon lime juice
1 dash bitters

Stir with ice and strain into cocktail glass.

IDEAL MARTINI

4 parts gin
1 part dry vermouth
2 parts grapefruit juice
1 part sugar syrup

Shake with ice and strain into cocktail glass.

INTERNATIONAL

5 parts gin
1 part dry vermouth
A few dashes Pernod

Stir with ice and strain into cocktail glass.

IRISH MARTINI

3 parts vodka
1 part Celtic Crossing liqueur
Lemon twist

Shake with ice, and pour into a martini glass. Garnish with a lemon twist.

May you be in Heaven a half hour
Before the devil knows you're dead.

Irish Toast

J. Edgar Hoovertini

Gin or vodka
Vermouth to taste
Stuffed olive

Shake gin or vodka with cracked ice, and pour into martini glass. Add the stuffed olive "bug."

Can you trust that man's martini? Hal Lipset testified in a 1965 Subcommittee hearing that he and his colleagues had developed small microphones and transmitters to replace the pimientos in olives, and had buried tiny copper antennas inside the swizzles. A handheld martini could work the room, recording snippets of conversation, or could be left at tables where people assumed they had privacy. Pretend that your Hoovertini is "bugged."

Java Martini

Vodka
Touch of Sambuca liqueur
Espresso coffee beans

After trickling vodka through ice chips into your favorite martini glass, stir in some Sambuca. Drop in a hard little espresso bean. When you get to the end of your drink it may remind you of black coffee and the morning after. Should this be your last drink? Bottoms up!

They say that a Martini is like a woman's breast. One ain't enough and three is too many.

Cocktail waitress, in the movie
The Parallax View (1974)

JOURNALIST'S COCKTAIL

2 ounces gin
Dash of fresh lime juice
Dash of bitters
Dash of triple sec
Dash of sweet vermouth
Dash of dry vermouth

Shake with cracked ice and strain into a chilled cocktail glass.

Before I start to write, I always treat myself to a nice dry martini. Just one, to give me the courage to get started. After that, I am on my own.

E. B. White

KNOCKOUT

1 ounce light rum
1 ounce vodka
1 ounce amaretto
Dash of lemon soda
Dash of grenadine
Dash of gin
1 ounce pineapple juice

Shake or stir all ingredients except pineapple juice with cracked ice and strain into a chilled cocktail glass. Stir in pineapple juice.

When made with technical precision, it's a TKO!

KUNDALINI MARTINI

Vodka to taste
1 whole black fig
2 teaspoons finely chopped ginger
Pinch of nutmeg
2 teaspoons honey
1/3 cup ruby port
1/3 cup simple syrup
1/2 peeled orange
1/2 peeled pear

Blend, do not liquefy, with a mixer and chill in refrigerator. Add vodka from the freezer to taste. You can experiment with all kinds of local fresh fruit as it comes into season. The fresher the fruit the more life force (prana) gets channeled through those energy centers (chakras).

LAMB'S CLUB MARTINI

4 parts gin
1 part dry vermouth
2 or 3 dashes Benedictine per drink

Stir with ice and strain into cocktail glass.

Add twist of lemon peel.

MADRID MARTINI

5 parts vanilla vodka
2 parts Licor 43 Spanish liqueur
1 part light crème de cacao

Shake with cracked ice and strain into martini glass. Serve after dinner.

That's no bull!

MANGO MARTINI

3 parts vodka
2 parts unsweetened mango juice

Stir with cracked ice and strain into a chilled cocktail glass. Garnish with a slice of mango.

Because Supreme Court Justice Charles Henry Truax was getting fat, his doctor, according to *The Dictionary of American Food and Drink*, told him to quit drinking martinis. The bartender at The Manhattan Club mixed up a little consolation and named it after the club.

THE MANHATTAN— A MARTINI LITE?

4 parts Canadian whisky
1 part sweet vermouth
1 dash bitters
Maraschino cherry

Pour into a cocktail glass over ice or straight up. Only 170 calories. And there's always diet cola.

MARSALA

1 part gin
1 part dry vermouth
1 part dry Marsala
Lemon garnish

Shake or stir liquid ingredients with cracked ice and strain into a chilled cocktail glass. Add lemon garnish.

MARTINI ROYALE

2 parts gin
Champagne

Pour chilled gin into a chilled cocktail glass. Top with chilled champagne, and garnish with a twist of lemon peel.

That's cool!

MÉDOC MARTINI

4 parts gin
1 part Cordial Médoc
Dash of dry vermouth

Stir with cracked ice and strain into a chilled cocktail glass.

Garnish with a twist of lemon peel.

MIDNIGHT MARTINI

6 parts vodka
1 part coffee liqueur
1 part triple sec or orange liqueur

Stir with cracked ice and strain into a chilled cocktail glass.

Garnish with an orange slice.

MINT MARTINI

3 parts vodka
2 parts peppermint liqueur

Stir with cracked ice and strain into chilled cocktail glass.

Garnish with a peppermint stick or sprig of fresh mint.

Perfect for the holidays!

MOCKATINI
(THE PRETENDER)

Tablespoon lemon or lime juice
Cup of tonic water

You don't drink, you are the designated driver, you are just a kid, or you've called it quits for the night? You deserve something refreshing and pretty—right now. Stir the above ingredients with ice and strain into a martini glass. Garnish with the usual green olive, lemon twist, or maybe a gold star.

Would you care for a martini, Mr. Babcock?
Would you care for an olive?
Auntie Mame says olives take up
too much room in a little glass.

Auntie Mame's 10-year-old nephew
mixes a martini for a straitlaced bank trustee,
in the movie *Auntie Mame* (1958)

MONKEY GLAND

5 parts gin
2 parts orange juice
1 part grenadine
1 or 2 dashes Pernod

Shake with ice and strain into chilled cocktail glass.

MUDDY MARTINI

1 part vodka
1 part Frangelico
Dash of Kahlua

Strain ingredients through ice into your favorite martini glass and say "Here's mud in your eye!" Popular during Prohibition, this boastful toast refers to horse racing, where the winner kicks mud into the faces of the losers (both two-legged and four-legged).

Nutty Martini

5 parts vodka
1 part Frangelico

Stir with cracked ice and strain into a chilled cocktail glass.

Garnish with a twist of orange peel.

Paisley Martini

4 parts gin
1 part white vermouth
Dash of scotch
1 lemon twist

Shake or stir liquid ingredients with cracked ice, and strain into a chilled cocktail glass. Add twist of lemon peel. Remember to drink it, don't wear it.

PARISIAN

4 parts gin
2 parts white vermouth
1 part crème de cassis

Stir with cracked ice and strain into a chilled cocktail glass.

How about seventy-three dry martinis?

Ernest Hemingway, to the startled assistant manager of the Ritz Hotel, as he escorted a boisterous crowd of soldiers and/or journalists into the lobby after the Liberation of Paris (1944)

PICTURE PERFECT MARTINI

8 parts gin
1 part red vermouth
1 part white vermouth
Cherry or lemon peel

Stir the liquid ingredients over cracked ice, strain into a cocktail glass, and garnish with a cherry or a lemon peel. Serve it straight up or on the rocks on a bad hair day. Forget the zit on your chin. Attitude is beautiful.

PINEAPPLE FLIRTINI

1 part vodka
1 part champagne
Splash of pineapple juice

Stir with cracked ice and strain into a chilled cocktail glass.

Garnish with a pineapple slice.

PRINCESS MARTINI

1 part vodka
Splash of strawberry liqueur

Stir with cracked ice and strain into a chilled cocktail glass.

Garnish with a twist of orange peel.

A VODKA INFUSION

You can find dozens of flavored vodkas for sale, but it is easy to make your own infusions. Just mash up vanilla beans, horseradish, jalapeño, pineapple, or whatever, and stick it through the neck of your bottle of vodka. Leave bottle in the refrigerator for at least a week before trying out your invention. (The longer it sits, the more flavor gets absorbed.) When you like the way it tastes (assuming there is some left), strain the liquid through a coffee filter and store in a freshly sterilized bottle.

PUMPKIN MARTINI

3 parts spiced pumpkin vodka
1 part Amaretto

Pour the chilled mixture into a glass rimmed with pumpkin pie spices and garnish with toasted pumpkin seeds or bits of old fashioned candy corn.

PURPLE HAZE

3 parts lemon vodka
1 part Chambord
Splash of 7-Up

Shake the lemon vodka and Chambord frantically to a Jimi Hendrix CD, but don't smash anything. Strain into a chilled cocktail glass and splash on the soda.

Okay, now turn down the volume and drink to the tune of *Smoke Gets in Your Eyes*.

RUBY MARTINI

3 parts vodka
1 part cranberry juice
1 part blue Curaçao

Stir with cracked ice and strain into a chilled cocktail glass.

Looks beautiful. Tastes even better!

RUBYREDTINI

3 parts gin
1 part white vermouth
1 part cherry brandy
Squeeze of fresh lime juice

Shake or stir with cracked ice, and strain into a chilled cocktail glass. Click your heels together and drink it at home, while repeating, "There's no place like home; no, there's no place like home."

RUMQUAT

4 parts gin
2 parts light rum
1 part dry vermouth

Stir with cracked ice and strain into chilled cocktail glass. Garnish with kumquat.

SAKETINI

2 parts lemon vodka
3 parts sake
Dash of cranberry juice
Dash of grapefruit juice
Cucumber slices and carrot

Combine all liquids in a shaker filled with ice. Shake well, strain into glass, and garnish with very thin slices of cucumber capped with a knob of carrot.

SAKE-TO-ME

6 parts gin
1 part sake

Stir with cracked ice and strain into a chilled cocktail glass. Garnish with a slice of fresh cucumber.

Banzai!

SAPPHIRE MARTINI

3 parts Bombay Sapphire Gin (renowned for
*   its spicy flavor)*
1 part blue Curaçao liqueur

Stir with cracked ice and strain into a chilled cocktail glass.

Garnish with chilled blueberries or crystallized violets.

SLOE GIN MARTINI

3 parts sloe gin
Dash of orange bitters
1 part white vermouth

Sloe is a type of berry, not a speed advisory.
This drink goes down pretty quickly. Hurry
up, and stir one over ice right now.

SUSHI-TINI

4 parts vodka
1 part dry vermouth

Shake with cracked ice and strain into a
chilled martini glass.

Drop in an olive stuffed with wasabi.

SWEET RUSSIAN

3 parts vodka
1 part crème de cacao

Shake with ice and strain into chilled cocktail glass.

TEQUINI

6 parts young tequila
1 part dry vermouth
1 dash orange bitters
1 dash fresh lime juice
Lime twist

Shake liquid ingredients with ice, strain, and pour into cocktail glass. Add a lime twist.

Aye, carumba!

TOOTSIE ROLL

6 parts vodka
1 part chocolate liqueur
1 part Grand Marnier

Shake or stir with cracked ice and strain into a chilled cocktail glass. For a swizzle, try a chocolate straw. Garnish with orange peel.

WAVE

3 parts vodka
1 part dry vermouth
1 part Campari
Lemon twist

Shake or stir liquid ingredients with cracked ice, and strain into a chilled cocktail glass. Garnish with lemon twist.

WEMBLEY

1 part white vermouth
1 part pineapple juice
1 part scotch

Shake or stir with cracked ice, and strain into a chilled cocktail glass. Garnish with pineapple.

WINDEX

3 parts vodka
1 part triple sec
1 part blue Curaçao

Shake or stir with cracked ice, and strain into a chilled cocktail glass.

YOLANDA

2 parts red vermouth
1 part anisette
1 part brandy
1 part gin
Dash of grenadine

Shake or stir with cracked ice, and strain into a chilled cocktail glass. Garnish with twist of orange peel.

ZUCCHINI MARTINI

Want to know what to do with those baseball-bat-sized zucchinis that take over the garden each summer? Make them into soup, ratatouille, bread, cake, and casseroles. The zucchini martini never caught on.

the morning after

*One martini, two martini,
three martini, floor...*

Seen on a cocktail napkin

HANGOVERS

HANGOVER HELPERS. A hangover is dehydration, low blood sugar, and mild alcohol poisoning. Not a pretty sight. Sure, torture yourself—swallow raw eggs, drink triple strength coffee, and stand under a shower of ice water. It won't do any good.

PREVENTION:

- Plan the number of drinks you intend to have and stick to your limit.
- Eat before, during, and after the party; it fills your stomach and slows the absorption of the alcohol. (No one said this was a diet book.)

    Alternate a glass of water or juice with each alcoholic beverage.

- At the bar, avoid the salty snacks that make you so thirsty you end up having just one more.

- Drink as much water as you can before going to bed.

- Don't drink more alcohol ("hair of the dog"). Your poor liver already has all the toxic metabolites it can handle, and it doesn't help anyway.
- Take a multivitamin.
- Drink water, soft drinks, and fruit juice.

  Sleep it off.

DESPERATION: People will try anything to escape morning-after misery. They:

- Rub sliced lemons under armpits (a homeopathic remedy, popular in Puerto Rico).

- Eat a small amount of horse brain (ancient Chinese).

- Drink cabbage water (ancient Egyptians).

- Have some bitter almonds and raw eel (Middle Ages).

- Take warm milk with a teaspoon of soot (19th-century chimney sweeps).

- Swallow warm urine (India).

What do you think of these suggestions?

If the headache would only precede the
intoxication, alcoholism would be a virtue.

Dylan Thomas

Martini Noir

GIN AND VODKA ARE OFTEN KIND TO THOSE WHO DRINK MODERATELY, and slow to punish those who drink too much. George Burns took two martinis before every performance and thrived for just over a hundred years. W. C. Fields managed to dazzle everyone with his brilliant comedy for many years before those gin breakfasts, chased by two quarts of martini mix every day, took him down. (His self-administered sobriety test was to balance a full martini glass on top of his head.)

It often seems Benjamin Franklin was right when he said there are more old drunks than old doctors.

But the martini does have its dark side. Jack London died from alcoholism at the age of 40, Dorothy Parker's wit didn't save her from its damage, and Sherwood Anderson died in 1941 after swallowing the toothpick in his martini olive.

The last shot of the day on a movie set used to be called "The Martini Shot," and Humphrey Bogart's last words were "I should never have switched from scotch to martinis."

Martinis taste good, and can make you feel better. But remember that they are powerful agents. Don't drive drunk, don't eat your swizzle stick, and get help if drinking becomes a problem. Just be sure that "The Martini Shot" never becomes your last act.

I know I'm not going to live forever, and neither are you, but until my furlough here on earth is revoked, I should like to elbow aside the established pieties and raise my martini glass in salute to the moral arts of pleasure.

Bob Shacochis, *Drinking, Smoking & Screwing*

[A]ll the charming and beautiful things, from the Song of Songs to bouillabaisse, and from the nine Beethoven symphonies to the martini cocktail, have been given to humanity by men who, when the hour came, turned from tap water to something with color in it, and more in it than mere oxygen and hydrogen.

H. L. Mencken

INDEX